Praise for *Eggtooth*

Jesse Nathan's singular vision and genius locate us in opulent lyrics that enhance our meager real-world experience into songs of radiance and wonder. Here is the Gerard Manley Hopkins of the 21st-century: poignant and sprung, and here are eminently Orphic poems written to reverberate through the ages.

— Major Jackson

I love the poems in *Eggtooth*. I love their knife's edge temporal and moral balancing. I love the way they call the bluff on citified notions of pastoral. I love the way they make me see anew.

— Linda Gregerson

A tour de force. Here poetry is a pleasure, a thrill …

— Fady Joudah

I can't think of another writer who so clearly sees the land for what it is: the actual organ from which we emerge and whose fate is directly linked to our own full sensory and emotional experience.

— Marie Mutsuki Mockett

Excellent ... Both lavishly granular and as expansive as the 'wildered sky' ... Sensuous pleasures and fresh revelations ... A significant new voice.

— *Publisher's Weekly*
starred review

An outstanding book of pastoral poetry from an impressive new voice. Nathan is a masterful poet — his language is vivid and alive.

— *Kirkus Reviews*

By turns finely wrought and bracingly direct ... alert to the wonderful and terrible things that happen beneath our feet. Nathan's ear for language and eye for the intersection of natural splendor and trauma are informed by his youth ... melding self-aware metaphor with age-old rigor.

— Kevin Canfield
The San Francisco Chronicle

If John Donne 'makes one little room an everywhere,' Nathan makes everywhere fit into his intricate rooms. His Kansas poems itemize local idioms and dignify minor moments with word-painting, impasto-thick. His triple-rhymed cadences make him an unusually melodious and affirmative elegist. *[Eggtooth]* is a tuning fork of regional sonorities, but it's also the original 'call' to poetry, still singing out 'personal and clear,' no matter how long the distance.

— Christopher Spaide
Poetry Foundation

The first thing one notices when one reads a Jesse Nathan poem is: one's body humming along to the music of his words ... the meaning lives in the music here ... That is, *Eggtooth's* music is so fresh, on both the micro and macro level, as the sound plays a live role in Nathan's explorations of memory, his various investigations into ecology, into poetics of place, into history. There's a generous variousness to this poet's lyric impulse. *Eggtooth* is not an ordinary debut but something quite different.

— Ilya Kaminsky
McSweeney's

Nathan attends to every sound. He wants us to chew our food thoroughly before we swallow, in the tradition of meticulous makers such as Emily Dickinson and her offspring Heather McHugh and Lisa Russ Spaar. Savor it.

— Ron Slate
On the Seawall

Ornate, highly musical, finding a kind of Marianne Moore-ish delight in expansive description ... My favorite moments are those when Nathan's speaker (that bookish boy) confronts his queerness ... Nathan's delight in stretching the bounds of our common ecologies of language, in trying to describe something until words are exhausted, might be called devotion.

— Amelia Ada
West Branch

[Eggtooth] is attentive and observant ... Powerful ... A work of mystical observations.

— Nick Ripatrazone
The Millions

Gorgeous ... a new sort of sting ... as concentrated with meaning as it is with sound. The drama in this 'growth of a poet's mind' is in the language. Nathan's style resembles those most sonically extravagant of poets writing in English who retain the power of narrative, from Gerard Manley Hopkins and Hart Crane to John Berryman and (more recently) Atsuro Riley.

— Katie Peterson
The Adroit Journal

Remarkable ... ambitious ... Here's to our eggteeth.

— Noelle Canty
Southern Humanities Review

Eggtooth

Eggtooth Jesse Nathan

ed.
UNBOUND EDITION PRESS
Atlanta

Copyright © 2023 by Jesse Nathan
Frontispiece © 2023 by Ian Huebert

All Rights Reserved

FIRST EDITION

Printed in the United States of America

LIBRARY OF CONGRESS RECORD

Name: Nathan, Jesse, 1983— author.
Title: Eggtooth / Jesse Nathan.
Edition: First edition.
Published: Atlanta : Unbound Edition Press, 2023.

LCCN: 2022951874
LCCN Permalink: https://lccn.loc.gov/2022951874
ISBN: 979-8-9892333-3-5 (fine softcover)

Designed by Eleanor Safe and Joseph Floresca
Frontispiece by Ian Huebert
Printed by Bookmobile, Minneapolis, MN
Distributed by Itasca Books

123456789

Unbound Edition Press
1270 Caroline Street, Suite D120
Box 448
Atlanta, GA 30307

for love

Contents

Foreword by Robert Hass   i

Straw Refrain   1

I

Dame's Rocket   5
A Country Funeral   6
Boy with Thorn   7
How We Played   8
Justin: Independence Day   10
A Note on the Cooking   11
In Those Parts   12
Scouts   13
The Stray   15

The Freak Speaks	16
Winter Scene	17
Footwashers	18
In a Churchyard After Dark, with Ruth	20
Goodbye at Monument Rocks	22
Clear as a Dream	23
If You Draw Rightly on a Wound, It Might Righten	24
What the Cedar May Have Said	25

II

Between States	29

III

Orphic	43
The Well, Rural Route 1 Box 43	44
First Love Song	45
Shock	46

Pastoral	48
The Whole Poop	49
Eggtooth	50

IV

Archilochus	55

V

Love and Ink	63
What Ruth May Have Wondered	64
Aubade Within Aubade	67
March	70
Coastal	72
Irena	73
Transplant	74
Yardlight	75
Postcard	76

City Beach	77
Canary Island Date Palm	78
Song on the Distance	79
What the Farmer Said	80
What Justin Said	81
When It Was Justin	85
Persephone	86
The Student	87
My Irena	88
Walking (With You) in a Field at Dawn	89

Coda

This Long Distance	93
Notes	97
Acknowledgments	100

Eggtooth

Jesse Nathan's *Eggtooth:* Making It New

How to speak about this brilliant and unexpected book? My impulse is mainly to point — look at this and look at this — and get out of the way. One of the pleasures of a new book of poems, especially a first book, is to turn to the first pages of it to see how the poet has gone about presenting themself. So here is the first stanza of the first poem in Jesse Nathan's *Eggtooth:*

>   Young gray cat puddled under the boxwood,
> only the eyes alert. Appressed to dirt. That hiss
>   the hiss of grasses hissing *What should*
> *What should.* Blank road shimmers. On days like this,
>   my mind, you hardly
>   seem to be.
>   On days like these.

   First of all, pure music: the rhyme on "alert" and "dirt," and the delicious and unusual word "appressed" to get at the languor of the cat in the summer heat, and the way the s's in "appressed" are picked up by the s's in hiss, and the over-the-top repetition of "hiss," "hiss," and "hissing" and the way they end by rhyming with "this," a word designed to put us in an immediate present. And the way the rhyme on "this" and "hiss" makes you notice that you have been reading a quatrain with an a-b-a-b rhyme scheme. And the way the quatrain devolves into a triplet rhyme on the "e" sound in "hardly" and "be" and "these." And the way the "e" rhymes seem to transform the "this" of things into the "these" of things, changing a moment into days, into the languor of summer and the blank road's shimmer.

i

My next thought was that this is gorgeous writing, and that, though there are in the emerging generation of American poets a considerable number of very interesting poets working from a range of aesthetic commitments, no one I can think of is writing quite like this. At times it reads like the packed and modulated music of early modernism, of — say — the young Hart Crane of *White Buildings*. And there are things I found myself charmed by — the poet's address to his own mind, even as it seems to dwindle to nothing in the heat and the short-line rhymes. And who does triple rhymes in English in the twenty-first century? It's the idiom of songwriters, Ira Gershwin and Cole Porter and Bob Dylan. It seems to belong to that kind of bravura playfulness. And I noticed and loved the fact that the only thing in the scene that isn't immobilized is the cat's eyes. They are "alert." The poet's mind may be going, but the cat's isn't. That's why it's under the boxwood hedge. It's hunting. And, sure enough, three of the local bird species show up in the poem's third and final stanza. Which led me to another thought, that the poem is so much about what it's about — a place and a time, and also consciousness — that you hardly notice the way it's written. It has fused its matter and manner entirely.

I'll save the third stanza for your inspection, but to see a little more of what he's doing in the poem, here is the middle stanza:

> No, no. See that sidelong silver drum? That hiss's a sigh
> of the propane tank. Two o'clock, you can smell it.
> Don't breathe that sigh. The creek's gone dry.
> Summer as wide as this wildered sky, days like this.
>   My mind, you hardly
>   seem to be.
>   Straw-frail, no breeze —

More music. This time abundant internal rhyme added to the end-rhyme, and it occurs, just as the subject of the poem, or at least its location, comes clear. A propane tank: we're in a rural place, in fact, as we'll find out as the book proceeds, in rural Kansas in the middle of the country in the summer heat. And this information comes up at the moment when the poet is correcting an impression. Doing that, revising the report on what is being seen — "Once again," Wordsworth wrote, "I see these hedge-rows, hardly hedge-rows, little lines / Of sportive wood run wild" — brings the reader to a peculiar intimacy with the speaker in a poem.

"Straw Refrain" is offered as a kind of opening note to the book. The first poem in the first section, "Dame's Rocket" shifts gears stylistically. It's a poem about a plant, in relatively short lines, a twenty-first century free verse poem in the twentieth-century manner of William Carlos Williams, the sentences disposed elegantly into phrases in the rhythm of speech, the diction of spoken English — "they say," "what's left." It's the principal medium of American poetry for the last hundred years, and the subject tells us what "Straw Refrain" suggested. This is going to be a poetry of place:

> Rising straight as canes
> around the older farms, the hairy leaves,
> little arms, the seed for jays,
> the fragrance a marriage
> of lilac and rose.
> They say it came with the early whites
> before escaping,
> as ornaments may,

the farmyards and gardens
for what's left of the prairie,
congregating sometimes in ditches
or among century hedgerows,
outliving towns
called Empire and Cicero.

    Dame's rocket is in the mustard family, with flowers like phlox. They like disturbed ground and they grow all over Kansas, and, something between a weed and a wildflower, as the poem says, they are not native to North America. They're European, escaped from gardens. There is a lovely ecological and historical alertness throughout Nathan's poems, and it's evident here. Dame's rocket. What a funny name, an English name from a time when rockets were fireworks and "dame" a dainty epithet from Mother Goose. And, he observes, this colonial has become a plant of ditches and hedgerows, outliving some of the towns to which the colonizers gave names full of classical resonance. There is something resonant, too, about the phrase "older farms." Like "century hedgerows," another European term, it calls up a past that is also called up by "what's left of the prairie," because Kansas had been a sea of deep-rooted prairie grasses before the plow tore it open to plant the grains that made people dream of towns named Empire. And the people who brought dame's rocket also brought their culture, and that gets reflected in the metaphor of marriage and the way the plants are seen to congregate.
    The next poem, "A Country Funeral" returns us to the rhymed seven-line stanza and introduces us to the culture of the place. Here is how it begins:

> The breeze, quick-footed, skims the beards of wheat
> trailing its hem over yellowing tassels
>   with a gliding so cruel for appearing so free
> as it blows through a hog-tight bull-strong fascicle
>   of shelterbelt planted to revoke
>   its force and flow —
>   *We've no polished phrases to recite, no*
>
> — our sung phrases reel on it, righten to a chord-plan —
> — *Abide with me, free us to grieve* —
>   and I'm nine, taking mama's hand ...

So much to admire in this writing. If you want to be taken well inside this country, wheat-growing southcentral Kansas, the land, the weather, the crops, the radical simplicity of the old European protestant sects at their ritual of burying the dead, and fixing it in the form of a transmission to a child's hand from the mother's, it's hard for me to see how you could do better, more magically than this. What won me on first reading was that "hog-tight bull-strong fascicle / of shelterbelt" — music I imagine Seamus Heaney would have loved, or Basil Bunting — and what amazed me was what came after, as if it were one of those haiku that seem to sum up entirely a certain view of life — "a gravedigger with no sleeves / smokes in the gravel lot / by his backhoe on a mat" — then managing to rhyme "lot" with "mat" and "thought" because the gravedigger, while the congregation sings their plain hymns of grief, is "hearing his own thought."

The next poem — and then I will stop paging through the opening sequence — "Boy With Thorn" is a single stanza long, and acts out comically the evolutionary meditation on plants and people that has been introduced, reminding us at the same time that in the deepest parts of memory our connection to place is apt to be embedded in the memory of bee stings, scraped knees, allergies, and in this case the really vicious thorns on locust trees. Which is why to write about place in a particular way is, as Wordsworth observed, to write about childhood —

> Wedged in my plantar fascia's rivers
> of tissue, the tip of a spike from the locust
> tree — some long as a boning knife — whose
> thorn evolved to ward off long gone
> mammoths, and who's
> yet to realize
> their absence.

— and remind us that some things rhyme and some things don't. Which is captured in the way that the s sound in "who's" and "realize" and "absence" sort of rhymes and sort of doesn't. And this may be the point when some readers, mainly those with an interest in technique, figure out where Nathan's stanza comes from. (He informs us later in the book.) It's one of the stanza forms John Donne invented early in the seventeenth century, around the time the English began to colonize North America, for his book of songs and sonnets. Here's the first stanza of his "The Good Morrow":

> I wonder, by my troth, what thou and I
> Did, till we loved? Were we not weaned till then?
> But sucked on country pleasures, childishly?

Or snorted we in the Seven Sleepers' den?
'Twas so, but this: all pleasures fancies be.
If ever any beauty I did see,
Which I desired, and got, 'twas but a dream of thee.

I will leave it to readers to identify what Nathan gets from this echo and borrowing. My sense is that it registers at the level of sound the way everything is like and not like everything else; it creates an ecosystem of echoic effects. Fascinating to see what he does with this stanza as a musical theme as he moves in the later part of the book from Kansas to San Francisco (as if it were a move from the prosody of Donne to the prosody of Kenneth Rexroth). "Between States," one of the two long poems in the book, begins in the Donne stanza and evolves into something like the free verse of Ezra Pound's *Pisan Cantos* as it tracks the history and ecology of middle Kansas —

and I'm imagining
these stinging nettles in my path

electrify my shins, imagining my stanza standing
for the grid within me, while my lines run on
like creeks across pastures, beneath a huge sun
of remembering, already halved by the line of the land,
land half imagined, half vanished
as a fog comes
not upon the earth but out of it.

It's an ambulatory poem. Something like the landscape-surveying English poems of the seventeenth century, something like an Australian walkabout, and something like Hart Crane's "Indiana," it is an entirely memorable hymn and elegy to, and accounting for, his ancestors' part in colonizing the prairie. I think it's quite remarkable the way he does it. He introduces aboriginal America by thinking about wind:

> describing a people who must've had scores of words for
> *zephyr*, people who (say the translators) could sing, "My children,
>   when at first I liked the whites, my children, when at first
> I liked the whites I gave them fruits, my children,"
>   a people whom the white government
> sent surveyors to to establish a trail's way
>   through these parts (my aunt used to sing
>   "When the prince wants an apple, he takes the tree ...")
>
> and the envoy arrived in that grass sea
>   to wheedle the Osage and the Kaw,
>   offering them $800 and a few saddles
> for a promise of permanent free passage. Local trapper
>   as translator. He the best
>   they could scare up, his Kaw sketchy at best, and I'm imagining
>   my relatives soon flooding in
>   with cabinet and poppyseed,
>   bonnet and springtooth, hope chest and hedgerow,
>   their book full of martyrs, dear as a mirror
>   and quilts made in the drunkard's path

       by hands that wouldn't hold a drink, obsessed and kind
selectively, women and men enough of whom
          must've believed when they were told to
              hallucinate a past to quell a present, told
"These are the Gardens of the Desert, these / The unshorn
           fields, boundless," in blank
    verse it was home to "a race, that long has
passed away" "in a forgotten language, and old tunes," "all is
       gone" though the actual act of emptying
          was actually still happening
     even as they set to plowing (that first time like plowing
       a doormat, the sod rent open
         with a sound like a zipper)
    harrowing, reaping, shocking, threshing,
   which is to say by 1846 the Kaw
were penned in reserves ...

The quotations come from William Cullen Bryant's poem of 1832, "The Prairies," a quite beautiful amnesiac account of the great plains in the blank verse of his master Wordsworth. The poem sits near the beginning of most anthologies of American poetry.

    (It's interesting to think about the very different forms of Protestant sensibility in American poetry — Emily Dickinson working endless changes on the hymn stanza, Walt Whitman's Quaker mother and his way with the rhythms of the King James, Wallace Stevens and the practical disposition of his Pennsylvania Dutch ancestors, Hilda Dolittle and her Moravian Brethren (very near to Anabaptist roots), or the pacifism of William

Stafford, another Kansan, and the Church of the Brethren. It makes one reflect on the fact that the Anabaptist sects, like Jewish culture, had to be profoundly conservative to survive at all the centuries of persecution they had to endure, and conservative in a way that also made for maverick and radical traditions. This isn't explicit in these poems except here and there — a relative counseling a Mennonite boy from one side of Turkey Creek that it's best not to marry a Mennonite girl from the other side of the creek — but it is an undercurrent to the book's themes of rooting and uprooting.)

Jesse Nathan was born in Berkeley, California. Both his parents are attorneys, who met in the 1970s working for Cesar Chavez and the United Farm Workers. His father is Jewish, from a little steel town north of Pittsburgh, his mother a Mennonite from Kansas. When he was a child, his parents, in part influenced like many in their generation by books like Wendell Berry's *The Unsettling of America* and Wes Jackson's *New Roots for Agriculture,* moved to his mother's home territory and began farming organically for wheat, eventually also setting up a mediation practice rooted in principles of restorative justice. The move was a decision that gave the young Nathan the world with which *Eggtooth* is saturated.

Mennonite central Kansas: the Mennonites were one of several Anabaptist sects that emerged from the Protestant Reformation. Anabaptists, according to one historical account, "were the unwanted and unloved stepchild of the mainline reformers, all of whom disavowed responsibility for their unruly offspring." Along with the Amish, the Hutterites, the Brethren, and a few other groups, they were the most troublesome to political authority. Adult baptism, nonviolence, a refusal to swear oaths, technological skepticism, community, simplicity — they found many ways to challenge state authority and they were persecuted relentlessly. One of the books that came with them from Europe was a seventeenth-century account of their collective suffering called *The Martyrs' Mirror.* Some of the Mennonites of Kansas, at least Nathan's part of Kansas, had their origins in Switzerland. But persecuted there, they moved east and set to farming in Ukraine, and farmed there for a century before they were told they were going to be subject to a military draft, and that was how German-speaking Swiss farmers from Russia (or the Russian Ukraine) ended up in Kansas.

Eggtooth doesn't tell us much about Mennonite theology or spiritual practice. There is a wonderfully odd description of a footwashing ceremony, but mostly the early poems are about, made out of, an intense, sensual sense of place. Nathan's mother's grandfather was the president of Bethel College, the Mennonite school that Nathan attended, and one of his Mennonite uncles was a prominent theologian. But *Eggtooth*, as its title implies, is a book about growing up, a book — as Wordsworth would have it — about the growth of a poet's mind. There is the farm, and there is high school, self-consciousness — "There was a boy even stranger than I was," he writes in "Scouts" — sexual experimentation, along with the storms and spiderwebs. So the latter part of the book is, among other things, the narrative of the narrator's leaving with a lover, who also belongs to the Mennonite world, to make a life together in the city. It's also — in "Aubade Within Aubade" the figure is a minus tide at Ocean Beach in San Francisco — the story of the dissolution of that relationship, and the beginning of another. And it is thrilling to watch him move in and out of his intricate stanza and various kinds and shapes of free verse in the telling that brings him to the urban poet writing this book.

Another of the pleasures of a new book is to turn to the end to see where it has taken you or what the poet has managed by way of a summation. Nathan ends with "This Long Distance," a poem in which the speaker, living now in the Sunset District, is on the phone with his parents:

> And the son, not really sure what then to say,
> says an iconic radio tower, from where he sits, presents
> like a comb jelly. And they, who in his imagination
> are in the dining room he knows well, hold up their phone, up against
> the back window to let him hear
> the call — so personal and clear —
> of the train out there.

It is a perfect image of the moebius strip of desire: to be homesick for the sound that called you away from home.

— ROBERT HASS

Straw Refrain

   Young gray cat puddled under the boxwood,
only the eyes alert. Appressed to dirt. That hiss
   the hiss of grasses hissing *What should
What should*. Blank road shimmers. On days like this,
      my mind, you hardly
        seem to be.
      On days like these.

   No, no. See that sidelong silver drum? That hiss's a sigh
of the propane tank. Two o'clock, you can smell it.
   Don't breathe that sigh. The creek's gone dry.
Summer as wide as this wildered sky, days like this.
      My mind, you hardly
        seem to be.
      Straw-frail, no breeze —

   You had a theory that the birds would silence
on a day like this. But the mocker's keenness
   and the kingbird and the vireos commence
to warble on as heat bears down a day like this
      my mind. You hardly
        seem to be.
      You road, you creek.

I

Dame's Rocket

Rising straight as canes
around the older farms, the hairy leaves
little arms, the seed for jays,
the fragrance a marriage
of lilac and rose.
They say it came with the early whites
before escaping,
as ornaments may,
the farmyards and gardens
for what's left of the prairie,
congregating sometimes in ditches,
or among century hedgerows,
outliving towns
called Empire and Cicero.

A Country Funeral

    The breeze, quick-footed, skims the beards of wheat
trailing its hem over yellowing tassels
   with a gliding so cruel for appearing so free
as it blows through a hog-tight bull-strong fascicle
     of shelterbelt planted to revoke
       its force and flow —
We've no polished phrases to recite, no

  — our sung phrases reel on it, righten to a chord-plan —
— *Abide with me, free us to grieve* —
   and I'm nine, taking mama's hand,
far thunderheads preach, and a gravedigger with no sleeves
     smokes in the gravel lot
      by his backhoe on a mat
     — hearing, but hearing his own thought.

   Then a windless, a wild calm. Four cousins boost
the yarrow-strewn coffin — *walk in us* — their lighthouse eyes
  — *O have you not heard* — show their charge is loose,
the body — *O fount* — sliding around as one misguides it,
     as virga near and curtain the creek.
      When dirt raps the casket, she squeezes
      my hand. It aches for reach.

Boy With Thorn

    Wedged in my plantar fascia's rivers
of tissue, the tip of a spike from the locust
    tree — some long as a boning knife — whose
thorn evolved to ward off long gone
        mammoths, and who's
           yet to realize
        their absence.

How We Played

Summer

 Home after an afternoon, say, goosing uncle's cranky catamaran
across the pixie humor of the reservoir's surface.
 Corker of a day. Sunset melting on its pan.
I drink from the spigot by the well, and it beards me in a watery lace.
   Mom salts ice in the wooden bucket
    of nostalgia, and we all crank the cream till its stuck
   paddles stop their play. And speechless, eat our luck.

Fall

 A lull: I trust that interval. Trust any spell to talk unhasty talk,
to breathe in unpredicted spaciousness. Time to voice what we can.
 Trust I was — am — that boy who'd lope and stalk
across the frosty fields with the dog, play at random
   turning into circles, running wider
    and wilder as dog chasing boy inspires
   boy chasing dog chasing boy to a scrum in a mire.

Winter

  Or if, by December, there wasn't any snow, we'd make a house
in the hayloft, craving a haven, a confine, a burrow —
   inside I'd fashion a table of bales, a brother or cousin
rig up two flashlights — our alcove of meanwhile
      disguised as three months' hay for the horses
        within which we'd run tunnels that start on the floor,
       seem to go deeper but turn up up out through a portal

Spring

  erupting on top of the stack. And when the redbuds turned pink
Justin would take me out setting lines — and so this doesn't balloon
   further, let me note how catfish and bass approved of our bait,
how midnights chest-deep in streams we'd tie it to roots,
     globs of baloney or gizzard or minnow. Sleep till six
       on a cot, wake to the trilling of wristwatch alarm clocks.
       Wade in, find fish. Later find leeches on our balls, tiny purple socks.

Justin: Independence Day

    We set up red and white striped tents in parking lots
after the harvest and before the plow.
    Wares with names like *Smoke Bomb, Night Stalker,
Bad Granny, Lightning*. A little extra income,
        a family affair. *Smiling from Ear to Ear.*
          We raise up our tents once a year
in parking lots. Eldest child — me — cashier.

A Note on the Cooking

   The state of my garden's a sign of my health,
says my mother the teacher-farmer. If plush, she's hale.
   If weeds, the classroom's got her head. Of her sometime wealth
of basil and pepper, rows of green beans, even broccoli, kale —
       a treat, she taught, to get to eat one's fortunes raw.
         As the asparagus toppled against her knife, I saw
      the stalks melt like some elysian butter-straw.

In Those Parts

    A voice insists *manure brings flowers*
but also *the more you stir it, the more you stink.*
    Sometimes the voice says, *In the heart, a fire —*
in the head, smoke. Other times
> *Who knows why birds go barefoot.*
> Or says, *Words pay no toll.*
Yet also
> > *Speak so I can see you.*

Scouts

There was a boy even stranger than I was
who'd call me in the evening
to see if I'd come to Scouts. Something in me
hesitated. Then one morning

during eighth grade English we got hall passes
and did it in a stall in the bathroom
taking turns over the john,
as thrilling as clumsy.

We kept our secret.
But he came to seem a target
around that one-light town. The cut of his hair
or the way he laughed, or maybe

his jittery hunched-up walk.
For a while he went on calling me
to see if I'd go with him to Scouts.
Instead I learned: treat him low

or be treated so myself.
Once in Art while the others snickered
I planted tacks across his chair,
and he sat down and shot up so quick

the chair sprang backwards, a few silver tacks
still sticking in his rear, his roar
like the shining in the corners of his eyes,
snarling as he came at me with scissors,

and only the teacher's lightning maneuver
kept me from my due.
After that he looked at me, if at all, like the traitor
I was. Later that year his dad moved him

to a Christian school where they teach
the planet was made in seven actual days
and dinosaur bones got planted by God
to amuse geologists and children.

The Stray

   Sunflowers like skinny men with rubberneck looks.
Spidery cloud keeping quite still. A lean, willful son:
   I care for the farm cats with straw and warm milk.
I'm about to see cruelty is the will's idiom
        if conscience isn't,
      I'm home after sore hours
    at school, a bouquet of slurs and scowls

   wilting in my hand, and here's the stray, a blue cat
mewling, sticking to me, always sticking
   like a burr on my sweatpants, and I spin on it,
hiss, but it won't leave off. And when the thing
       was done — by my hand, hell —
      a sick-sweet smell
     of what I can't tell.

The Freak Speaks

    To be silent, he says, as a radiant
fig-fat spider, star in her spokes of wire
   across an empty stall, glinting garden giant
linking bags of peat to spade to tractor's flat tire
      above a drain that's centered in the floor
         of a gripped-in-ivy wing of the barn, built for
       milking, fitted with a wide sliding door —

    To be silent in that musty ease, he says, calls up the zest
I there relieved once for a monster dog with a monster sex
   perking his tail and gently snorting, possessed
as mosquitoes drink my cheeks, my calves, my neck —

Winter Scene

    Gunshots knock like pool balls in far fields.
Or more like someone knocking on a board.
   Remnants of husks click click mealy
and delicate babble the spirits of spent corn.
       A hawk, red-vested, dabbles
          sideways resembling a bag
      on the draft, then jags

   over cedars we put in in September.
One made it. Lining the road, the rusted
  stems and plastic flags seem to remember
the others. At four, the yardlight's light appears cuspid,
       neon, like a greenish wick.
          In the farmhouse, time over the sink ticks
       and the snake plant's spear-tip

       dribbles dewbells
        of sap.

Footwashers

> The waiting and dreamed-of ritual grace ...
> — Valerie Weaver-Zercher

  Stout as a dancehall, white clapboard and square
it stood between fields a short piece from town,
  bordered by gravel, abut by God's acre —
this roominess anchored by pews. Through which wound
     Mother in her special vamps
       and Daddy in his monkstraps
     to where a line of basins wait,

  warmish water lapping and the linen towels drape
where feet of different walks have gathered, foot-foundered
  and fit alike, for each soul to cradle, douse, and bathe
their righthand neighbor's heel, instep, digits found
     immaculate or blooming lint
      or faint funk or toenail paint.
     Footloose, nailmangled, imp —

   most everybody's here. There's Auntie, who pronounces it
play-zure as she communes with Sue the drama coach,
     and Uncle, who keeps fake owls in his garden, who quizzes
Tom the sheriff (who's ticklish) as he sprinkles his toes,
         and down-at-heel Justin, who yesterday
            hunted mallards up a slough, splays
         his shovels to a wingtipped banker,

   and there — there I am, turning over a word
in my head — *catenary* — for parabolas that fountains
   form, word for the U a necklace makes, curve
an upside-down arch, as I towel off a sprouting
       cousin's fallen arches, anklebone,
          all thirty-three joints known and unknown
      that carry me away from home.

In a Churchyard After Dark, with Ruth

   She grins and says *medium*, meaning sometimes she sees
downy feathers floating by, or gets a gust of mums
   overcoming doorways, or a tingle in the feet
or hears a faint *ting* of bell. Ruth, to whom the elements fess up
      as if sleep were a tide
         on which their voices glide,
      sometimes whistling, sometimes shy.

   She told me she'd learned of an aura's light
as it blanketed her brother, who, yanked into a baler,
   flew out ribbons. Her father broke. Took flight
touring country churches, as though to brawl with failure.
      Became an anti-sin magician.
        I see her idling at his show: thin,
      looking luminous but slightly hidden

in back of the sanctuary. I smile, I think only half thinking,
and she waves, and drifts over. Gets to telling me
  how her brother suffered, how it led her blinking
here with her father and his fierce faith. "I see,"
    I say, itchy-eared, lip-lolled, availed,
      available and unveiled —
    it must've been obvious how I quailed —

"Do you" — she sniffs — "ever sense your dead?"
I must've flinched. Must've nodded. We sidle out
  (gliding somehow, somehow free by her side)
to lounge in a burr oak's buttress-root couch.
    At some point I ask her what he
      who was her brother says. She seems
    to read the air. "Don't saint me."

Goodbye at Monument Rocks

    Layer on layer these did not grow
so much as gradually remain. Eyeless river, long
   lost, cut these spires from the chalks just so,
left embrasures like portals for travelers in a song,
        and cut turret, cut skyline
           of limestone, cut shrine
           hemmed like my margin's line.

    Tumbleweed hesitates, hooked on a cow patty's
crushed rose of coffee. Rock a variation on ginger.
   Clumps of purple gayfeather, a.k.a. blazing
star, indicative of overgrazing. Little visions.
        Clam, sharktooth, lily crinoid,
           ram's-horn ammonoid —
        cliff-faces that keep a lizard employed.

    And when we leave them in the rearview mirror
she murmurs *Clear as a dream*, she almost
   singsongs it, on her mind her father's
speech at our goodbye, his close
        breath through the phone,
           his mounting howl, the tone
        like wind through dusty stones.

Clear as a Dream

    She looks on as I say hello
and hears her father's teary echo
    as he presses me please to look out
for his baby girl. Who's no doubt
        not a baby, not a girl,
           not his or his world's.
        We hang up. She does a twirl.

If You Draw Rightly on a Wound, It Might Righten

And so? And so they drive over arid floors
of long-departed seas, and up with the land's ramp
   off the continental shield. They witness the mural
of mountains emerge, and they span the North Platte
      near the train-bridge trusses,
         career in the wind-boom of trucks
      through basin, past bluff —

Straight through? No, no, they stop at a tattooist's hut.
What for? Why, to mark themselves for themselves.
  Is it their first? Yes, and they — *What is it of?*
He gets a barn-swallow. She gets a spiral.
      Where? His shoulder, her ankle. *And what
         do they mean?* So many questions. I don't know, but
      ink as blue as bruises may be a kind of trust

  sealed and believed. *And does it hurt?*
Of course. It seeps with dewdrops of blood —
  Why did they do it? Charm? Armor? Maybe certain
pain is meditative. *Are they happy?* Well, they have a long hug …
      And after that? They drive till they arrive
        at the city. Soft sky, trees mighty,
     busy bridges festooning the night.

What the Cedar May Have Said

If I were half as free as you
I wouldn't droop,
make faces of parchment,
shed branches like phantoms,
wouldn't hide
a heart of soft scarlet.

If you were half as free as me
you wouldn't go —
you who leave not once, like guests,
but over and over, like friends.

II

Between States

[Walking the creek. Springtime.]

   I'm remembering it took twenty minutes
for the local firefighters to reach us the night the lightning
   got the attic blazing. Long enough to take a bath. I'm remembering
as the road-grader growls by somewhere, its unremitting blade
      leveling the sand of a road,
         bunched and rutted,
      stopping the land from taking it back —

   stopping it in the language of a straight line.
And I'm remembering how someone used to toss
   Busch Lite empties down our crushed-limestone drive,
thrown from a passing pickup, cans silver-glossed
      azure and partially crushed.
        Imagining the hush
     of the creekbed in winter's crust,

   ice sounding off. But it's April and April is stinging nettles,
sneezeweed and terse breezes, wide-awake-skies, vein-blue tulips —
   I'm remembering a rainstorm mudding the road even as I pedaled
home, left the bike, ran soaking through fields following the lips
      of the waterway that appeared,
        articulate, weirdly
      lit-up in lightning. Imagining Roma my grandmother heard

    in that pasture as a child, they would canvass the farmhouse,
barter for milk. At dusk the calls of their children. Imagining
  people before that who tracked this route, maybe camped
on these banks, fished, called out to a friend
     a strategy or result. Could eat what they caught
without second thought. I'm remembering
         the placard in the half-ring
      of fading pines off Old 81

describing a people who must've had scores of words for
zephyr, people who (say the translators) could sing, "My children,
  when at first I liked the whites, my children, when at first
I liked the whites I gave them fruits, my children,"
  a people whom the white government
sent surveyors to to establish a trail's way
        through these parts (my aunt used to sing
       "When the prince wants an apple, he takes the tree ...")

and the envoy arrived in that grass sea
   to wheedle the Osage and the Kaw,
   offering $800 and a few saddles
for a promise of permanent free passage. Local trapper
      as translator. He the best
   they could scare up, his Kaw sketchy at best, and I'm imagining
     my relatives soon flooding in
        with cabinet and poppyseed,

bonnet and springtooth, hope chest and hedgerow,
    their book full of martyrs, dear as a mirror
    and quilts made in the drunkard's path
    by hands that wouldn't hold a drink, obsessed and kind
selectively, women and men enough of whom
        must've believed when they were told to
            hallucinate a past to quell a present, told
"These are the Gardens of the Desert, these / The unshorn
          fields, boundless," in blank
      verse it was home to "a race, that long has
passed away" "in a forgotten language, and old tunes," "all is
      gone" though the actual act of emptying
        was actually still happening
      even as they set to plowing (that first time like plowing
      a doormat, the sod rent open
      with a sound like a zipper)
    harrowing, reaping, shocking, threshing,
    which is to say by 1846 the Kaw
were penned in reserves, by 1873 pushed out of state, and by 1876
      ("Boundaries. Forced marches. Monoculture …")
my foreparents by the powers
  are granted swaths of so-called open land
      to open up, and I'm imagining, first of all, much water
  under no bridges, the streams like this they would've seen
      foaming with fish, peppered with turtle, an opus of birdsong
        they'd have heard, and maybe heard also of two men

    who set out from the northeast border
killing 800 wolves before they reached the Smoky Hill River,
    and I'm seeing buffalo
   (10,000 killed in one hunt in 1882 by men with Sharps)
   as I watch a black bull corral the herd
in the paddock I'm threading through,
 whose hump is a massif, whose head is
  low so his body's like a grader,
 the droves rambunctious and nervous as they quick-march,
  they must've heard me in the underbrush
  or they've heard and seen that Gleaner,
road-bound dust comet
  traversing one of these little concrete (lime and clay) bridges
   that's all the speaking these roads and creeks
  are wont to do with one another.

And when it's gone, and the cattle gone, and the air cleaner,
 the quietude I think not "strange and empty," the creek
   not foaming with dace, but cocoa-brown
    with topsoil, the ground
   greened over by recent rain, a clown-

 faced cloud somersaulting slowly as a contrail
punctures her nose, plane proving a scratch
 that dissolves on the cosmic glass, frail
trace of cities, I'm down here imagining the chaff

      in the air of olden times
        and a people, my
    mother's, who must've believed the line

  that these contours were theirs to grid, grounds theirs "years /
before" they landed this "gift outright" blank "still unstoried, artless,
unenhanced" for the taking
   like a creeper takes that cottonwood
  by the ears, takes what it wants, while still giving
 an impression of peace to a poet
  having a sit before he blunders on with his eclogue,
passing not through a prairie, not
through a woodland, but through a *prairie woodland*
   (technical term for this band of life, woods along streams
     surrounded by oceans of grass,
   I'm remembering the way, flying in, the creeks seem to cross
  the gridded roads like veins drawn over graph paper)
 which natives and settlers relied on, spotted afar, to locate
    what water there was
  among networks of vines and tough shrubs
that clinch these muddy lips,
  this mustache of canopied verdure running a few feet on either
bank, a curt succession
  from lovegrass, dropseed, bluestem, to great big trees
  rising from "abominable desolation"
where "nothing points" though it happens to be home

to lady's slipper and pheasant and kingfisher and windmill-grass
and what are states to them? What are states
to bobcat and nitrogen-eating bacteria and dung beetle
and racerunner and sunflower, to carpets of sorghum, beans,
cornfields replete with large centipedish machines, woodland
a slender band of betweenness, whose meandering logic
seems but is not whimsy through the subsoil.   Of course
this state already had a song. Had "revery," had "chants going forth"
like how the Pawnee would sing before battle,
"Let us see, is this real,
let us see, is this real,
let us see, is this real,
this life that I am living?"

I'm looking where a log points, a slippery log
that makes its point over the real froth
as I waver on it between real banks to the real knob
the trunk lands on, this land of lightning bug and common gray moth,
of the misnamed prairie dog
not canine but squirrel, the meadowlark not
any kind of lark, the horntoad not

toad but spiked lizard, the jack rabbit truly a hare,
the prairie chicken truly a grouse, the locust
a false acacia, even the buffalo were
really a species of bison, but in their crush

        to have and sow the place
           I can picture the settlers' pinkish faces
           and sometime glee as they attach their names

to things like *catlinite*, pipestone, maroon erratic
   tracked in on the feet of glaciers crushing spruce forests,
     used (and called what?) by First Peoples
   for carving pipes, fine-grained, soft,
     picked up by my loner grandma
        who'd pick over roadsides, scour the gravel drive
     for wheatsized one-celled fusulinids, searching them out
   as if divinities slept in minerals, in chips
 of meteorite and sharkteeth,
and I'm remembering that it wasn't the land that carved me apart,
  but a system of culture, a school of
flak from an elder if you couldn't pull a straight furrow,
   whose term for the leftover corners
   of wheat left standing at the cambered angle
of a turning combine's path
   was *jews*. I'm remembering someone saying he hadn't
  done his jews yet. And I'm imagining the neighbor in a CASE hat
sweating as he forces the waterway in his field
  to flow straight, trenches out the curves, tautens the meander
   to get a few more acres of arable land. *Plow
    the dew under,* went the old saying. Meaning
get out there early and turn the soil, a culture

    of extraction displacing itself, its sports teams
      called the Pipeliners and the Threshers,
  the wells failing, the farms drying up, the schools
      consolidating, and I'm remembering mine was a school of
milk all over my locker, of laying tacks on an outcast's chair,
  the usual cruelty with a rural edge,
    remembering that I, who got kicked in the spine,
  had my own complicities
in the unstated contract of "freaks for export only" —

    all that projected emptiness. Only the land was always a solace.
      I recall it as I cross now under a bridge at the bend
        in the road that was Empire, cattle town, "erased," felt one
      newcomer to the prairie, "blotted out" — I've always loved
    that unroomed vertigo, a sky that swallows you —
and I hear again the grader hacking
    somewhere back around the section, his angled blade
  a balm to the quadrangle's party,
    which gave us passable roads and the persistence of windmills,
  he's following the latticework his ancestors laid
over branchings of stream and river
    (which look from above like leafless trees
      or paint peeling, or like cracks in a wall)
  "Eternal prairie and grass, with occasional groups of trees,
Frémont prefers this
to every other landscape," Charles Preuss

wrote on their way to taking California, "To me
it's as if someone would prefer a book
of blank pages," and always
I want to linger in those pages
but I'm imagining the "tension

between singing and the journey," remembering
people I knew who worked red-eyes
at the hatchery in the nearby dying town, who'd brag
of killing runts in creative ways, knocking them to slime,
Candace, Carmen, and the Hacker boys,
figures grown up with
who don't know what figures they seem

for whiteness and sex and bored destruction, I'm remembering
some uncle saying, *Best not to marry
on the other side of the creek* —
but I say a border is also a world,
zone of cottonwood hackberry luxurious weeds towering
and scarcely a human presence, a golden haze
where monarchs lunge and bounce
in private liberated gloom
that must from above look like giant

interlocking hooks, I'm imagining the bobolink's view
who flies with the aid of the stars,

    how a month ago the stream was ice,
how an hour ago a mare was stretching her neck
      over barbed-wire fences
        for the sweeter grass, and I'm imagining
    these stinging nettles in my path

    electrify my shins, imagining my stanza standing
for the grid within me, while my lines run on
    like creeks across pastures, beneath a huge sun
of remembering, already halved by the line of the land,
      land half imagined, half vanished
        as a fog comes
    not upon the earth but out of it.

III

Orphic

    His noiseless blooming in the callous earth. I followed
a drybone branch, spiderweb-cracked, off the Running Turkey.
    Under a no-name concrete bridge. Fusty, sallow,
skeletal bass, half-sunk in rock-mud, mouth open to the murk ...
        Driftless one, did you drown in air
          as you guarded last fry? Did you glare
        as your pool was slowly not there?

The Well, Rural Route 1 Box 43

    What wasn't hidden wasn't plainly there.
Year by year I tracked our well's steel-capped PVC-pipe
   headpost leaning vaguely as it disappeared
in cedar-shrub, growing palisade, evergreen and tight.
        I liked to crawl back and stare
           into the source, rampant for cool air
      ushering up, signal of elsewhere.

    Elsewhere — under three feet soil, ground up
by glacier, laid on clay fourteen times thicker, world-making drab
   stacked on twenty feet sand, loam, lost downs,
next a lake in shale, no eye sees it, shifty slab
        in its bed, and trilobites pressed
           in their portraits of absence.
        I'd pry up the flap and disinter cobwebs.

    I'd pry up the plywood, startle the ages with a blast
of my flashlight's skittering light.
   Didn't know then I was looking at a past
alive in the must and crushed in layers. A spider twitches.
        Easy to see from her stance
           she understands chance.
        Inhale that dank, sweet expanse.

First Love Song

You were never like the poets,
windy-eyed behind their open windows,
making notes before they knew
how dear the cost.

You taught me how to hear
summer on the rain,
and the wind came flapping through it,
and I gaped, unafraid.

Shock

    As the storm moved in, I watched the night sky
before I slept. A biblical clap woke the house
   to sprays of sheetrock, a powdered sprite
springing from the nailheads. Air flavored with ozone.
      In the hallway on the ceiling, a halo
         grew orange around a fixture, aglow —
    and Dad on the phone

   downstairs, and now shepherding the young ones
out to shelter in the soaphouse, and Mom, who's usually
   sharp as a crack, fumbling in the pandemonium
at the extinguisher — so I, small and spry,
      someways slithered in
        up the crawlspace, and
    find a burning fan.

Not just that fire-fanged attic fan. Wire, floor, rags,
even wall-studs chuckle in those flames.
   A company that almost comforts. Until I gag
on smoke or fear, and jerk the pin and aim
        a sweep of foam
          blond as bone
     until it's dark and I'm alone.

   Some say it was lightning in a mineral bisque
that triggered first life. Grandpa said in 1933
   he lost six head — his life savings — to one strike.
And I, in the soaphouse later with an EMT,
       would sense in the rafters swallows
         veer, loop, follow
     as if a shadow had a shadow.

Pastoral

    The anvil cloud, trundling away.
The smashed wet wheat, like a cat
   ambushed by a bath. The baby
birds strewn about. I step in what
       seems like a redwing
          under the swing —
      ants scramble out.

The Whole Poop

   In military slang, poop is the really valuable info.
As in, *Gimme the whole poop on the guy.*
   My uncle, who did a tour in the navy, says so
and I'm thinking about it as I clear the bindweed
        from the buffalo grass
           that slopes to the lagoon's mass
        of duckweed-topped morass

   forty feet in diameter, in depth maybe four
at the spot where egesta emerge to be chewed
   by ravenous aerobic beings. Sidelined and bored,
flies covet the slough of our selves, which stews
        abetted by wind, by the sun's touch,
           and works, it often does, without so much
        as a green whisper of stench

   from this, what couldn't take, our shit commons —
fiber, TP, buttons of crud, corn kernels of truth, liquid hosts
   where our productions focus, and peacefully break down
girded by a berm and a fence of hedge-apple posts.

        Somewhere in the pasture's air
           a meadowlark trills. I hear
        his song go down its stair.

Eggtooth

> Whose bread I eat, his note I sound.

And so at last spoke John Donne's ghost. Leaned up
out of my book and nearly bit me.
 "Seven," he says, "sponsors creation but
also vice. Three (and four) holy, but three
      marks the rooster's count." His face
       was gold, pounded thin. "I say
     use me like an eggtooth, break

  the shell that shields you, let me be the germ,
hoarder-of-calcium, the bulb of sharp
  caruncle, expression of beak (of horn)
that makes a toothlet to snout-thrust, a barb
      to barb what's chipped away
       by the very thing maintained
     and encased. Enamel glaze

  grades the puncturer's tool. Draw your breath
by drawing a hole. Use my imbalanced
  device, half-medieval, to shuck frank death
as you surge with goodbye. As you fast
      and breathe and pay,
       supposing the face a blade
      sustained to sing and to fly."

IV

Archilochus

Woke to a wind that rose full of birdcall
dropping it fresh as if drawn from a well.
Starlings mobbing elms like a creek talking.
Farmhouse window rattling lightly. My eyes
find my desk: notes and lists, tasks and numbers
interbedded with books stacked — like the beams
that used to be a soaphouse, now mythic
behind the barn — in dust, cord, silverfish
growing over clear intention. Love, I
woke to the wind that rose up full of birds
and for a second didn't know my name.
Woke with a tickle of panic, haunted
but not sure why. A thirsting to have
my sensibility immersed, drawn through
an othering element, though I think
he's a wretch. My job today is to dig
to put in a few posts, put in a fence,
and as I stab and sink my narrow spade
through turf and root and worm and sticky clay,
I'm thinking of boundaries, I'm thinking him
hooligan, scamp, soldier. Skilled at singing.

He traded cow for lyre. Joined an army
to feel sober, fatal. And in buskins

fought among medlars, where the wine waves lisp
Aegean sand lining the isle Thasos,
where marble quarries ziggurat down.
Lived by the ash-spear, liked screwing like war.
Seam of the scrotum, he sang. *Wick rubbed raw.*
Iamb a weapon. Myrtle, soft horn, grape.
One fragment reads simply, *rhinoceros.*
When his promised's father called it off,
he seduced her young sister in a poem
and came on her crotch in the last tercet.
Kept living by the promptings of his sex.
Said *need is a limb-loosener.* And then
of his poems crowed, *There's virtue in the feet!*
His were silenced by an acquaintance, Crow.
It was an all-out fight, we don't know why
Crow slashed him groin to throat, left him to rats.

His mom had been enslaved. His highborn dad
a founding father of a frontier town,
island spired with pines and arching from the sea
like an ass's backbone. He thought friends hurt
the most. That we were surely promised light.
That change is birth: metamorph, term of art
for stone's reception to — without melting —

great stress. In the fall heat, I plant these posts
till lunchtime. Sandwich of apple, turkey
sliced sheer as cheesecloth, on buttered wholegrain.
I hear George, my cabbie once in Athens:
Sure it's nice here, unless you want to leave.

Hypocrite. Greek for actor, answerer,
interpreter. When you read these drafts, love,
you frown. Say *so much anger in your lines.*
Anger? Is that it? With marble tongues and teeth
he'd adorned his escutcheon of wood,
it nictated in sunlight like sunlit seas —
I'm thinking of our work and what it means:
A fence may be a seam, or seem a bridge,
both are gestures in the air. This, a shield
so the dogs don't muck in the septic soup,
to separate what's slough from what runs free —
that's what I think I'm up to here? Maybe.

(Initiatory lust, remember when
you brought me here, nudged me down on bracken,
toiled on me like on a straw, gnats fussing ...
A pleasure went out through me like a gale

though *pleasure* is much too shallow a word
for what roils me like ribbons in a wind.
Some law, some ageless vise, had grip of me
and squeezed and squeezed, and wrang me fully out.)

It's so far back in time. The critics say
"we have no reason to believe he in
any sense ever reached home." Deserved
wasps hover on his gravesite. "The scold," what
Pindar called him. Horsetail-helmed, liver-tongued
and ever hard as stakes of Osage Orange.
Who hated the polish of frauds and hacks,
hated tasteless desire, boring dinners.
Overlook my ways, he'd say. *I'm countrified.*
Eat with my hands. Read naked in the stock tank.
Banned in Sparta for his candor. In Rome
all trainee-priests were forbidden his poems.

But to the Spartans, his lascivity
wasn't the obscenity. What burned them up
is just what carries me through unmoored months,
has carried me, and has to sound my poem
for one who had no epic in him, had

just one shot voice, a tetchy melody:
Who, as he tells it, bleeding on Thasos
in the screech of battle, perceives he loves
his life more than that fight, more than duty
to any reckless collectivity,
shrugs off his prized and perfectly good shield
because he can run faster without it,
and abandons those slopes, to start over.

V

Love and Ink

you'll cross the continent, confess
to angels of death —

you'll yawn, limp, squint, arrive in a U-Haul
sweat, rattle a typewriter, scratch paper,

a globe breaking at the equator —
and she'll tickle your feet

and you'll lick beneath her ear —
your legs jello, your penis a flower —

but your antiquated words will clatter away
and your romance

droop like two palms —
a jay will screech, a story itch —

What Ruth May Have Wondered

    Silence in the countryside gets so dense and so deep
it amasses body, untellable shape, heavy, larger
  in its nothingness. On windless evenings
it would wrap around us like a vast comforter.
      Your ears can ring from it,
        it seems a witness
         listening, swallowing itself.

    And if your mood is gentle, it is the gentlest cradle.
And if you're wheeling with fear of what might be,
  it's cousin to madness. Then again, later on
when we'd moved to the city, noises would heckle me
      as I slept, a motorcycle's bay
        blocks away zap me awake —
      or I'd lurch up to a siren's catwail,

  shuffle to a window to be amazed how few stars are there.
Starry-eyed love, old book I'm reading says, is flattering mischief.
  When he and I met, I lobbed him a fat apple for
his true smile, his strawlikeness, his bearded unbelief.
      I said I take my apples like onions,
        diced or fried, and my onions
        like apples, in hand, in smiles, raw —

and he says he likes raw, too — and then we're talking
with the dead we miss most, and necking against a tree.
   I savor his filthy wit. One reunion of his gawking
relatives, he deadpans on his way to the toilet *Gonna be*
       right back, got a package to post
          and I'm in stitches trying to keep my repose,
    keep my coffee out of my nose.

   Stitching we did by trading stories. His house
jacked by lightning, say, for the one about my father
  who caught me dancing (in pants!) and swore my blouse
fitter for the street. Or how that machine swallowed my brother.
       But now I get a creeping wonder
         that all we have in common is some other
          oceanic longing. That we're each other's plunder

or plain alibi. And, can he name his privilege? Shall I?
Why is it I'm in terms of *him* here? Where his projections read
  and misread the thoughts inside my head. And in my eyes?
Why won't he meet them when we're fucking?
       (I've read the natives in these parts
         gauged your stature by how far
       you could see, not how far you could fare.)

I know there's places on this earth where night goes on for months.
I'm asking for a steadiness that defies possession.
   A hand under my breast, he hoists me to his tongue
and tastes. Feels nice. But what's *not* a matter of address?
            One of us once said — I'm not sure
              who — I'll help you steer
            if you'll wake to tell me where.

Aubade Within Aubade

   The city proceeds for several miles and finally shivers
and slides into ocean empty-handed. Day's got its chin up
     on the watery prospect. They've paused where
the sand is wet slab, where the sand crabs grub.
         A minus tide, some call it,
          when the water's way out —
        venation of dried-out

   seafoam forming, islands of puddles, stranded isopods
and beach-hoppers circling in mochas of shoal.
   The gulls excited, strafing. Sponges, as though odd
donuts had been secreted from sand. In Ovid, there's a hole
       where a king's barber stuffs a secret
         but it babbles back, and begets
          muttering reeds, just like that.

   And just like that, *I'm leaving* is what she's intoning
as the sky turns ruddy and plural of cheek,
   and morning grows speechless with a glint in the foam
of muted outlying rumbling waves; crows, entreating —
       but as she speaks, for him it's three
         summers ago, the two of them sacking
       a honeycomb in the silo, smoking

   the bees out, getting tipsy on honey,
so garishly bonded in matte-finish sweetness.

Now she's muttering *I'm seeing* — a genre
beginning in darkness, flowing toward brightness,
    which is also an end, like candor —
        someone else. He thinks, *I'm no better*,
    thinks of a stranger,

    what started in a park, 2 AM — on a swingset,
on the slide — they'd moved to a bedroom, a twin bed
    among teetering cities of books, among which he
afterward woke to a siren, toppled those books, genitals
        still sticky, still flush. The call in old times
        of the nightwatch passing — *light! light!* —
    what supplied the *alba* its title

    to the lovers meant dawn, loathsome dawn nears, so
Flee! was in this case a firetruck charging down Mission ...
    What music his farmboots beat in the ears
of the empty sidewalks! Instinct drove rhythm
        up their dew-glossy stoop, instinct
            left dewprints,
        dawn an embarrassment

    mild and threatening — then he's under the covers.
Moments later she's home, off unexpectedly early,
    her breathing is breakers as she undoes her scrubs —
he acts long asleep. But she wants

    to go out, right now, out to the beach,
        I want to see —
    starfish exposed, gleaming

  riveted like spiders spotlit on a wall,
daybreak on a tide minus 1.2, and in the shallows a man
  in yellow waders casually culling
the mussels from unveiled stands
        of white-shat rocks
            usually way out in surf —
        bristly bunches, dripping clusters

  passive as teeth. *But tell me,* she asks, *something
secret —* and the culler makes quick specific motion —
  *Was that love we had, or just a stab at escaping
to some other newfound stranded emotion?*
        A fleck, a flash of aubergine.
        Clatters in a bucket. *So clean —*
    she trails off, her face to the rising sun.

March

There's a moment — barely — when you see both
ocean and bay from the 280 as it mills north
   near Millbrae, the waters flash what they know
of daylight, and you register being a sort of gliding porch
      before dunking back under cypress
         and their bob and sway, and the press
      of eucalyptus and acacia in full dress.

It was like that — like a shot — when the freeway
let the crying out. In a flash was what was trying
   to let a crying out, and if I hesitate to say
weep it's in mind of a celebrated novelist's sighing
      as he tells me he can't countenance
         a grown man of my (his) race
      writing *weep* with a straight face.

My face wettens. A bit of soul, maybe, exiting
the body. A disheveled, monkish tassel
   on a snowy egret on the evergreen exit sign
settles nothing. As I, hands on the wheel, unravel
      like that overflown yellow —
         bursting along a rural
      artery, atlas-line, mellow

concrete sentence of a path —
   the acacia's lemon bath
over the roadwall like over a dam.

Coastal

      I saw a seaside stair
        that might well go forever
   down, down into a lapping mightbe —
then I'm doing gainer, backflip, cannonball
   while sleep-dark houses sleep beyond the trees
that form around me both a shield and a pall,
      the stars some hard, far cry
        in the interrogated sky,
      and a satellite the only reply.

Irena

A woman fell through a rock
and traveled time
to be gathered in her story.
When I read it
in a sci-fi paperback
I found yellowing
in a house I slept at one night
driving through California,
I thought of Irena
somewhere dreaming, Irena
who says there's an accuracy
to nostalgia,
but no precision.
As was my pumpkin-faced nose
of yesterday to Irena Irena
Irena who wears a precision of dreads
high in a bundle
like a Thracian queen.

Transplant

    As from the sunk springtooth's rusty frame
they dig up me, they speak to me and to each other
  in tones of those who feel — feeling plain —
they've always known, and yet just met, the other.
        How now their gestures rhyme.
           Together lower me into slime
    and silt-slip, cold and fine,

  and cradle-place my fragrant, adaptable rootball
and bole where awl-leaves spring,
   immobile. I am the stuff of pencils.
Water beckons me to a new standing.
         She nibbles — he lets her — his earlobe
      as I sip the soil soaked by the hose,
        high-hearted and stunned to the root-toes.

Yardlight

    When you gave me the gift, it was as if
I was stumbling out behind the well
    where cedar fronds grow up thick,
as if I'd lit upon the metal box fixed to the pole,
        and nudged that hefty switch,
            and heard that satisfying hitch
        and hum of the footcandles' stitch.

Postcard

> I entered the universal, dazzled and desiring.
> — Czesław Miłosz

"Not a gathering," she says, "a *milieu*." She'd made cake,
orange cinnamon with dates, from a Tunisian recipe,
   and we savor it on a bench, lulling with midday
in a plaza of planetrees and fountains knee-deep,
       while strangers of a mind to meander
         meander. "Milieu," she muses, "from a term
   for medium plus a word

  for place." This in the place of the dog who sighs, asleep
in equable sunshine. Of the ukulele variations on *Over
   the Rainbow,* of the elder who styles a baggie
a glove to bus his Frenchie's ordure. Of the checkerspot
       breathing on the pollarded knees
        of a planetree, of the shaggy lady
   who lives in this commons. These

  commons of sand and cement, all the voices and feet
they've absorbed, all the rickety easels of nudes'
   sprawled amid strollers, trikes. Not a bleat
of car alarm. She wriggles free of her shoes.
       Remembers a coyote we've seen
         weaving through after dark, on a beat,
   pausing in the bandshell to sniff the concrete.

City Beach

> Most excellent is dignified leisure.
> — Cicero

We were watching the waves in their folding
from seats on the sand
  where the sea came boiling
then withdrew from the land.
      The dolphins like curds
        popping up in a soup
     on a glittering loop

  and ships going out, and ships coming in —
and then a woman came darting
  out of a car pulled over be-
hind us, pulled off her pants
      and undid her top, and kept on at top speed
        naked and fulgent and diving,
    and the pelicans cruising did not veer

    and her breasts were flying
      and the froth became her hair.

Canary Island Date Palm

Couldn't say the dream I had last night.

But I might start
by saying your dates
were motionless in a breeze,
almost orange like bittersweet,
almost yellow
like bittersweet.

Song on the Distance

a soaphouse in a cemetery

Stones have grown those green-brown beards
concealing fictions etched on chins,
  and scars of dates that steam obscurely
in my dreaming. In my dreaming we are singing
      to lose a disclaimed instinct —
        I'm pheasant, hawk, and goldfinch —
        and lines we would dispart with.

Dank as a well in a room called Night,
windows thick with grease and mist,
  alive in the shed where we boil the lye
while the fog a song — is it song? — enlists
      its wail over acres. I'm the green
        of fields the mind must be
      to tune a farmer's evening theme —

I'm bare as a lightbulb, those flickers and surges
and the filament that beams across it,
  its span a rallied urge's
catenary line, ours against the losses,
      as when two knees of land anticipate
        what a city-bordered bay —
        what a bridge — instates.

What the Farmer Said

   So I hear you're through. Had enough
of amber waves, etc. The situation stinks
  to high heaven, sure, the future feels rough.
'Course when I began, there seemed no way to shrink
        inputs and we were just
           absorbing what a bust
        our growth really was —

  still, I wager what some grew was more than greed.
A love, in my case, for the light on water in a fallow field.
  And I love my shoulders dressed with sunshine. Way nothing
interrupts the light out here except a far-off YIELD sign
        flashing as the sun dies,
           and then out come the lightning bugs
        and the powder stars of the countryside.

  Point being, I wish you'd reconsider. Stay
and be a saving remnant. Look, my rusted harrow
  already earthbound by volunteer cedars. No more *plow
the dew under.* New roots for a coalition of no
        to growth, no till, and prime
          to let the dew do its benign
        labor, as we retire timeworn lines.

                Stay on, won't you?

What Justin Said

Yesterday it seemed
here to Galva
on fire.

Velveteen ash. Made the sunset
an astonishing alibi. Goodbyes
are such blind spots.

The horse-headed oil pump
nods up and down, up and down.
Summer isn't finished

beating the hell from us.
Bindweed in the ditches
creeping into fields —

did you know our ancestors
brought it in their seed-wheat
from the old country?

Over my head a horde of gnats
forms a singing tower,
a story there too

if you can read it.
I read the roads
and the roads are visions

of liquid in the dog days.
Streaks of jets
stack and fade

and when the green header
of the John Deere
met the metal cradle

of the wheat truck
it made a call
like a hawk dying.

In a horn
the gold burst forth,
how many acres' worth

spilled
in the stubble,
and dad fuming to the house.

His mud clumps
a trail upstairs, I hear him now
flop down, Fox News.

I had a snout in the dream,
I was one in a pack
of raccoons. Purple diamonds

for eyes, we zombiewalk
long driveways
and the ruts of ethnic lanes

and get nailed
by tractor-trailers
or hail.

Did you know there's an ailing
in our wheat
known as *strawbreaker?*

I find bindweed
terribly pretty, that pearly cup,
that sand-dollar cloud —

but its roots unbridle
a stringy lightning,
a deep-choking system.

I'm unstrung, and I'm rakewhacked.
In two weeks, it's away
to law school. I'm missing

the whiff of anhydrous
already. Ha.
I trade this

for Socrates, certiorari,
habeas corpus, contortion
by torts.

When It Was Justin

   And then we lie still in our bluestem fortress.
Nearby are headstones, leaning and sinking.
   An apple in hand, a hat that reads SPORT —
"No what are you, really?" he asks like a sphinx.
       "That," I laugh, "is what the miser said
         when sophomore year I played
         the tight-lipped, no-faced

   Ghost of Christmas Future: remember my winging,
straight at Scrooge, one long-nailed finger?"
   A friendly tease is a pleasing thing.
I watch his teeth break the apple's skin,
       and with mineral glamor he arches a brow.
         "One year," I add, "I wore a cloud
         of beard and played the shouting

   cheddar-loving cruise-ship castaway — "
"Always," he asks, "bit parts?" "Always," I say, "a mask" —
   and he kisses me right on the lips. Cottonwood cotton
drifts on the draft like a pillow's been shot.
       "Once," I say, "they cast me as 'singer,'
         COUSIN ROY, COUNTRY SINGER
       WANNABE." His smile lingers.

Persephone

I saw quick rumps
leap from the cedar bower.
Maybe it was you
startled by a passing car—

sister of the fields,
globe-eyes and cloven feet,
little bearded repetitions of wheat
swallow your retreat.

The Student

                    of wonder a student of blunder.
Wonder and blunder, blunder and wonder
  I'd chant till I'd dulled any feel for either.
But a course had been set. Poppies, coral-color,
        shook out their bells on our rented yard.
           For her I planted those mums in that yard,
      at bills and paperwork I mumbled, alarmed.

  After bills and paperwork had worked us hard,
we stepped out for a smoke in our tiny yard
  and bumped small bells that hung in that yard
as if to confirm a course had been set. Poppy, coral —
      I'd chant till I'd dulled any feel for either,
        wonder to blunder, blunder to wonder,
     a student of blunders a student of wonders.

My Irena

Your amethyst earring
on the edge of an earthly sink, I inhale
your age of sage and pine, I inhale
a particularity that could eat
everything for a thousand years
like a collapsing star, some angel
of nervous light, our shape
in a mirror, a forest, a garden …
But nothing will stand in, nothing complete,
not even the coast road we took
until a rockslide halfway
closed the way, and what else to do
but pose with the ocean
behind us in its currents and distant liners
and a moon of pocked truths.

Walking (With You) in a Field at Dawn

They sashay, those tendrils of mist.
Sunlight glitters in the wet spiderwebs
draped all over the witches' broom
flaring from the base of the tree.

Hackberry, I think. Witches' broom
a flag of panic, a casting madly outward
under the stress of something
we can't see. The tree, the only one out here

and whatever secret fears it has, the swallows
still call its upper branches home.

Coda

This Long Distance

    Sunday, in his grandmother's time, had been the day
you went visiting. Noontime news, topped with beet borsht
    and pickled pigs' feet, cottage cheese stuffed in pancakes —
and schputting, silly talk — and coffee. His art,
       with his hopes, had conspired to conduct him
         many states away, but even now when
       Sunday's here he calls his kin.

    And when he'd call his parents, his dad would begin
with weather — *Five inches since Friday,*
  seven and three-tenths since Monday, it may even
hock up more — and his mother would inveigh,
      or other times dial up other composings —
        First frost came so we picked up the hoses,
     slid the barn door closed,

    any minute now we'll get fresh straw for the stalls —
or she'd say how they *butchered the hens, one had a clot*
  of new eggs in her, ready to lay — or she might tell
stories of Aunt Larrie who never married and carried a snuffbox,
      or dad would describe having recycled
        faxes that had blankened,
      each message returned

    to the ether, and then the son might describe a minus tide or tell
how his shoulder — tattooed — has haired over, as if his swallow

flies in a thicket, or he'd ask *How low is the well?*
or *Which kind of locust, again, is the swing tree?* — and so
     forth, they'd sneeze, cough, mention the soaphouse
        had had to be razed, or that the catamaran was trounced
in a squall, or how their bodies were giving out —

an organ recital, they call it, and he, drinking coffee, might offer
as balm the lights up the hills in the night in his city
  described as the winkings of great piles of embers,
and his mother might report on emerald leaves, emerald wheat,
     high leaning cloudbanks, or his father
      might say that the starlings were
    mustering the pasture, they could murder

    if they wanted. And the son, not really sure what then to say,
says an iconic radio tower, from where he sits, presents
  like a comb jelly. And they, who in his imagination
are in the dining room he knows well, hold up their phone, up against
     the back window to let him hear
       the call — so personal and clear —
     of the train out there.

Notes

A Country Funeral: "Abide With Me," "When Grief Is Raw," and "Oh, Have You Not Heard of that Beautiful Stream" are among the hymns they are singing. Virga, visible from a distance across the prairie, appear as streaks that seem attached to the underbelly of the clouds and fade near the ground. They look almost like hair.

Goodbye At Monument Rocks: Rising suddenly out of the plains not far from the Kansas-Colorado border, the chalk formations known as Monument Rocks were the first in the country designated by the federal government as a National Natural Landmark.

In **Between States,** material quoted but not attributed in the text comes from: an Arapaho Ghost-Dance song translated by James Mooney in 1896 ("My children ... "), William Cullen Bryant's poem "The Prairies" ("These are ... ," "a race ... ," "in a forgotten ... ," and "All is gone"), Amy Clampitt's poem "The Prairie" ("Boundaries ... "), Laura Ingalls Wilder's novel *Little House on the Prairie* ("strange and empty"), Robert Frost's "The Gift Outright" ("years ... ," "gift outright," "still unstoried ... "), W.H. Auden's "Bucolics," specifically the "Plains" section ("abominable desolation," "nothing points"), Emily Dickinson's "To make a prairie ... " ("revery"), Walt Whitman's "Starting from Paumanok" ("chants ... "), a Pawnee war song translated by Daniel Garrison Brinton in 1890 ("Let us see ... "), Carl Becker's essay "Kansas" (in this case the line has been abridged from "There is a saying here that freaks are raised for export only."), Willa Cather's *My Ántonia* ("erased," "blotted out"), and Raymond Williams's *The Country and the City* ("tension ... "). Books by William Least Heat-Moon *(PrairyErth)* and

Wes Jackson *(Altars of Unhewn Stone)* were invaluable resources in the making of this poem, as were the circulars published by the Kansas Geological Survey. The "large centipedish machines" are irrigation systems. A farmer — "the neighbor in the CASE hat" — who forces a stream in his field to flow straight does so because he figures it'll give him a few more bushels at harvest time. Straight lines he deems more efficient, and more suited to his machinery, than the meandering line the waterway makes. Turkey Creek was a dividing line in the community, separating two groups of Mennonites who, despite their many similarities, came from two different communities in Europe, communities that represented two different traditions, and who did not forget this fact in their new land.

Pastoral measures the effects of a spring storm in middle America. These are sometimes so violent that baby birds are tossed from their nests. Heavy rains often flatten crops.

The Whole Poop: The phrase "shit commons" is borrowed from a poem of that title by Jake Levine.

Eggtooth: Donne used variations on this stanza in a handful of early works, including "The Good Morrow," "Confined Love," and "Witchcraft by a Picture." Like the adagia of "In These Parts," or the axiom — "plow the dew under" — that appears in "Between States" and "What the Farmer Said," the epigraph here is a version of a local saying, originally spoken in a German or Swiss dialect, and translated with the help of the work of Isaias J. McCaffery.

Archilochus is indebted to the translations and writings of Guy Davenport, H.D. Rankin, and Roberto Calasso.

What Ruth May Have Wondered: In the sixth stanza, see N. Scott Momaday's observation about the Kiowa in *The Way to Rainy Mountain*.

Transplant: Hardy and good for windbreaks, the eastern red cedar is one of the few trees considered native to Kansas. Volunteers often come up in ditches, along train tracks, around refuse piles, and increasingly in the open prairie.

What Justin Said: Many farmers in the region would set the stubble on fire after the harvest as part of a process of readying the land for the next crop. After burning, they plow.

Acknowledgments

Thanks to the Andrew W. Mellon Foundation, Bread Loaf, the Ashbery Home School, the Community of Writers, the Kansas Arts Commission, and the Arts Research Center at UC Berkeley for support during the making of this book. I'm deeply grateful to the editors of the following magazines in which these poems first appeared, sometimes in different forms or under different titles:

> *American Poetry Review* ("Justin: Independence Day," "Scouts," "The Freak Speaks," "In a Churchyard After Dark, with Ruth," "Clear as a Dream," "Yardlight," "Postcard," and "Song on the Distance")
> *The Believer* ("Boy with Thorn")
> *BOMB* ("A Country Funeral," "First Love Song," "The Student")
> *Boston Review* ("First Love Song")
> *Brick* ("What the Farmer Said")
> *The Cortland Review* ("Transplant")
> *Fence* ("Orphic")
> *Harvard Review* ("Winter Scene")
> *Harvard Review Online* ("Eggtooth")
> *The Hopkins Review* ("City Beach")
> *The Journal of Mennonite Writing* ("What Justin Said")
> *Kenyon Review* ("Goodbye at Monument Rocks," "If You Draw Rightly ... ", and "The Well, Rural Route 1 Box 43")
> *The Land Report* ("Persephone")
> *Literary Matters* ("When It Was Justin")
> *The Los Angeles Review of Books* ("My Irena")

Michigan Quarterly Review ("Footwashers")
The Nation ("Love and Ink")
The New Republic ("Coastal")
The New York Review of Books ("What the Cedar May Have Said")
The Paris Review ("Straw Refrain" and "Shock")
PN Review ("The Whole Poop" and "Coastal")
Poetry London ("Between States")
Poetry Society of America ("What Ruth May Have Wondered")
Plume ("Love and Ink," "Canary Island Date Palm," and "Persephone")
Revel ("A Note on the Cooking," "Footwashers," and "Yardlight")
Smartish Pace ("Pastoral" and "Walking (With You) ...")
Subtropics ("Archilochus" and "Aubade Within Aubade")
Virginia Quarterly Review ("Orphic" and "March")
The Yale Review Online ("Dame's Rocket" and "This Long Distance")
Zyzzyva ("A Note on the Cooking")

"Eggtooth" was republished on the *Best American Poetry Blog*, ed. by David Lehman. "How We Played" was anthologized in *The Experiment Will Not Be Bound*, ed. by Peter Campion. "In Those Parts" was turned into a comic strip by Lauren Haldeman. Versions of "What Justin Said," "Irena," and "My Irena" were published by Jeff Alessandrelli in a chapbook called *Cloud 9,* and "My Irena" was also printed by Jesús Castillo in *Vertebrae*. A version of "Song on the Distance" was reprinted in *Mantis,* and a version of "What Justin Said" appeared in *Pacific Journal*. "The Well, Rural Route 1 Box 43" was included by David Baker in "Nature's Nature," a portfolio published in the *Kenyon Review*.

About the Author

Jesse Nathan was raised in northern California and rural Kansas. He teaches literature at UC Berkeley, and he was a founding editor of the McSweeney's Poetry Series. His poems have appeared in *The New York Review of Books, The Paris Review,* and *The New Republic.* This is his first book.

About the Type and Paper

Designed by Malou Verlomme of the Monotype Studio, Macklin is an elegant, high-contrast typeface. It has been designed purposely for more emotional appeal.

The concept for Macklin began with research on historical material from Britain and Europe dating to the beginning of the 19th century, specifically the work of Vincent Figgins. Verlomme pays respect to Figgins's work with Macklin, but pushes the family to a more contemporary place.

This book is printed on natural Rolland Enviro Book stock. The paper is 100 percent post-consumer sustainable fiber content and is FSC-certified.

Eggtooth was designed by Eleanor Safe and Joseph Floresca.

Unbound Edition Press champions honest, original voices. Committed to the power of writers who explore and illuminate the contemporary human condition, we publish collections of poetry, short fiction, and essays. Our publisher and editorial team aim to identify, develop, and defend authors who create thoughtfully challenging work which may not find a home with mainstream publishers. We are guided by a mission to respect and elevate emerging, under-appreciated, and marginalized authors, with a strong commitment to advancing LGBTQ+ and BIPOC voices. We are honored to make meaningful contributions to the literary arts by publishing their work.

unboundedition.com